My Jesus Storybook

My Jesus Storybook

Carrie Lou Goddard

Illustrated by Charles Cox

Abingdon Press
Nashville

To Carrie Ruth

A delightful and charming
young lady

ISBN 0-687-19924-7

Book Design by John R. Robinson

My Jesus Storybook

Contents

In a Warm Place for the Animals

The animals came to a large place at the end of the day. The cold wind could not blow on them there. There they were warm through the night.

At one side there was a manger where food was placed for the animals to eat.

One night Joseph and Mary came to the place.

They were tired.

They had traveled a long way.

They needed a place to rest.

They needed a place where the cold wind could not blow on them.

"We can stay here," Joseph said to Mary. "I will make a place for you to rest."

Mary was glad for a place and a time to rest.

In the quiet of the night something wonderful happened. A baby was born!

Mary wrapped her baby in the long cloths she had brought. She held the baby close in her arms. Mary loved the little baby.

Joseph saw the manger where food was placed for the animals.

"This will make a good bed for the baby," he said.

So Joseph cleaned the manger and made a bed for the baby.

Carefully he laid the sleeping baby in the manger. He loved the new baby.

Mary and Joseph looked at the baby as he slept. "What a wonderful baby," they thought. "We love him very much."

"His name will be Jesus," Joseph said.

"Yes," answered Mary. "His name is Jesus."

A Home for a Growing Boy

Mary and Joseph brought Jesus to their home in Nazareth. They were glad to be home.

They were glad for Jesus to be in his own home. "Jesus grows so fast," Mary said one day.

"Yes," Joseph answered. "Soon he will be big enough to help in the carpenter shop."

Each day Mary went to the well for water.

She was glad when Jesus was big enough to go with her. She walked slowly so he would not get behind.

The other women at the well smiled at the little boy.

"What a fine boy you have," they said.

"Yes," Mary answered. "We love him very much."

Each day Joseph went to his carpenter shop.

He used his tools.

He worked with the wood.

He made things for his neighbors.

Sometimes Joseph took Jesus with him to the carpenter shop.
Jesus liked the carpenter shop.
He liked to play in the wood shavings.
He liked to smell the fragrance of the cedar wood.
Most of all Jesus liked having Joseph talk with him.
Sometimes he would help Joseph with the work.
Jesus liked to be with Joseph.
"Someday I will be a grown-up man, too," Jesus thought.
Mary and Joseph were happy to see Jesus grow.
"We thank God for Jesus," they often thought. "He is growing in every way."

Children in a Meadow

Children were playing in the meadow.
They had come with their mothers and fathers.
They liked it here in the meadow.
They had space to play.

Other people were in the meadow. They were sitting with some men. One of the men was Jesus. He was talking to the people.

"Come, children," the mothers and fathers called softly. "Today we have come to the meadow for a special reason. We want you to meet the man who is talking to the people. His name is Jesus."

The children came with their parents. They walked toward the place where Jesus was sitting with his friends.

As they came closer to Jesus, some of his friends rose and walked toward the children and their parents.

"Do not come any closer," one of them said.

"There is no time for the children. The grown-ups need to hear what Jesus is saying."

The children were sad. Their parents were unhappy. They all turned to go away.

Jesus saw them going away. He called to the children and to their parents.

"Do not go away," he said. "I want to see you. Come closer to me. I want you to know of God's love and care. I will tell you about God."

The children and their parents began to smile.

They came close to Jesus.

Jesus smiled and talked with them.

He took some children in his arms.

The children liked being close to Jesus.

They liked the stories he told.

"Jesus loves us," the children thought. "We are important to him."

Jesus on the Hillside

One day Jesus was walking near a hill. He saw that grass was growing on the hillside.

He looked at the birds flying overhead.

Flowers were in bloom.

Jesus left the road and climbed up one side of the hill. He sat down on the hillside.

Jesus' friends climbed the hill and found places to sit near him. They loved Jesus and wanted to hear the stories he told.

Jesus looked at the people. They were waiting to hear what he had to say.

"Look at the birds," Jesus said. "When they are hungry they fly around looking for food."

The people saw some birds flying around.

Other birds were hopping about hunting for food.

"God planned that there would be birds in the world," Jesus said.

"Yes," the people thought. "God planned well for the birds. God cares for them."

"Look at the flowers," Jesus said.

The people looked at the flowers.

They saw some in full bloom.

Some only had buds.

Their leaves were green.

Their blossoms were bright and colorful.

"The roots of the flowers grow in soil," Jesus said. "They are watered by the rain. The sun shines on the leaves of flowers and helps them grow. Their blossoms are more beautiful than the clothing of a great king. God cares for the flowers."

"Yes," the people thought, "God planned well for the flowers. God cares for them."

"Look at the people on this hillside," Jesus said.

The people looked.

They saw mothers and fathers.

They saw grandmothers and grandfathers.

They saw young men and young women.

They saw children. Some were very small, and some were big

enough to run and play.

"God planned for people in the world," Jesus said.

"People can talk.

They can care for one another.

They can work.

God cares more for people than he cares for birds and flowers. People are important to God."

The people sat quietly thinking.

How wonderful that God had planned for each one of them.

"We are more important than birds and flowers," they said. "God cares for each one of us."

A Tree Beside the Road

One day Zacchaeus came along the road.
Zacchaeus was a man who lived in the city.
He was walking fast.
He looked at both sides of the road.
He saw a tall tree by the side of the road.
Zacchaeus ran to the tree.
He began to climb into its branches.
He sat on a branch so he could see the road.
He sat watching and waiting.
A group of people were coming along the road.
They were walking toward the city.
The people were walking with Jesus.
They were eager to hear the things he had to say.
Zacchaeus sat on the tree branch and watched the people and Jesus.
Jesus was the person he wanted to see.
He had heard many things about him.
He had heard that Jesus was a friend to everyone.

Zacchaeus needed a friend.

The people were under the very tree where he was sitting.

Jesus stopped and looked up into the tree.

"Zacchaeus," Jesus called. "Come down from the tree."

Zacchaeus came down. He stood looking at Jesus.

"Today," Jesus said. "I must talk with you. I must go to your home. I must eat food with you at your table."

Zacchaeus was very surprised.

He knew that people did not like him.

Only a few people ever came to his home to eat with him.

Jesus wanted to talk with him.

Jesus was going to his home.

Jesus was going to eat with him.

Zacchaeus was a very happy man.

Zacchaeus and Jesus walked together.

They talked with each other.

They ate together.

Zacchaeus thought, "This is a wonderful day for me. I have found a friend who likes me, who visits with me, who eats food at my table. I want to be this kind of friend to others."

"Jesus, I want to love others as you have loved me," Zacchaeus said to his new friend.

"I am glad you walked and talked with me. I am glad I could share food with you. I will do this for others. You are my friend."

From a Boat

Jesus was walking along the seashore.

He was alone.

He found a place to sit and rest.

People passing by saw Jesus sitting beside the sea.

This was their friend.

Some of the people came to sit, to ask questions, and to talk with him.

Others went to tell the news that Jesus was sitting beside the sea.

Men, women, and children came to sit with Jesus.

They crowded around him.

Each one was trying to get close enough to see Jesus and to hear what he was saying.

Jesus saw some fishermen near the water. They had a boat. Jesus called to the men. "Let me sit in your boat," he said.

The men were glad to have Jesus use their boat. They helped him into it.

The boat floated on the water.
The fishermen held it steady.
Now all the people could see and hear Jesus.
"I will tell you a story," Jesus said.
"Once a farmer had seeds to plant in his field.
The farmer used his hand to scatter the seeds.
Some of the seeds fell along the path.
The birds flying in the air could see them.
They flew down and ate the seeds.
Other seeds fell where there were many rocks and not much soil.
These seeds began to grow right away.
Because the soil was not deep the roots could not find water.
When the sun shone on them the plants died.
Other seeds fell in the places where the thorns grew.
When the thorns grew they were thick and tall.
There was no room for the seeds to grow.
Some seeds fell on the good soil.
These seeds began to grow.
They grew into strong and healthy plants.
These plants made many new seeds.

When harvest-time came the farmer gathered the grain from these seeds.

The farmer was glad.

Now he had grain to make bread for his family.

He could save some to plant next year."

The people listened.

They thought about the story Jesus had told.

"We will be careful to sow the seeds where the soil is good," they said.

Jesus watched as the people went to their homes.

He said, "Those who know and understand God's love for them will share it with others. They are like seed in good soil."

The Man on a Donkey's Back

Jesus and some of his friends were near the city of Jerusalem. Flowers were in bloom along the road and on the hills. Birds flew overhead. Sometimes they sang songs. The branches of the palm trees had fresh new leaves. It was a warm spring day.

Many persons were traveling along the roads into the city of Jerusalem. An important day was coming soon. It was a day for praising God and giving thanks. It was called Passover. The people were coming to Jerusalem for that special day.

Two of Jesus' friends went into a small town near the city. They walked until they found a yard where a donkey was tied. The donkey was young. No person had ever ridden on his back.

The two friends untied the donkey and led him out to the road where Jesus was walking. The men had brought the donkey so Jesus could ride on his back.

One of the men took off his long coat. Carefully he spread his coat over the donkey's back. "That will make a comfortable seat for Jesus," he said.

Jesus sat on the donkey's back.

With Jesus on his back the donkey walked along the road that went into the city. Jesus' friends gathered close around the donkey. They smiled as they walked along. It was a happy time.

Other people who were traveling along the road saw the man on the donkey. They began to move closer. "It is Jesus," they said. "He is our friend. We will walk with him into the city."

There were children walking along the road into the city. Some of them knew Jesus. They remembered the stories he had told. "There is our friend, Jesus," they called to one another.

The children came close and walked with the grown-ups around the donkey. The children clapped their hands. They sang, "Praise! Praise in the highest!"

The grown-ups smiled and sang with the children. Some of them gathered the green branches of the palm trees to wave in the air as Jesus rode by.

"This is our friend and teacher," the people called out.

By the time they arrived in the city there were many friends with Jesus. They were glad to be with him. They clapped their hands and sang: "Praise! Praise! Blessed is he that comes in the name of the Lord!"

That day Jesus had ridden into the city on a donkey's back. His friends had walked by his side. Some had waved palm branches. Many had clapped their hands and sung songs of praise. They had shown their love for Jesus.